# A Story of Our Own
*A Collection of Short Stories*

Glenn L. McDonald

Terri E. Lyons

L.T. Woody

Mario D. King

RYCJ

*Published by*
OSAAT Entertainment

OSAAT Entertainment
P.O. Box 1057
Bryn Mawr, Pennsylvania, 19010-7057
www.osaatent.com

All rights reserved.

No part of this book may be reproduced or transmitted in any form or by any means, graphic, electronic, or mechanical, including photocopying, recording, taping, or by any information storage retrieval system, without the written permission of the publisher.

First Edition.

To learn more visit www.osaatent.com

Copyright © 2015 Terri E. Lyons, L.T. Woody, Mario D. King, Glenn L. McDonald, RYCJ, A story of our own. Fiction – Short Stories

Cover Design by OSAAT Entertainment

Library of Congress Control Number: 2015918269

ISBN: 978-1-940994-00-0

Printed in the United States of America

*Dedicated to the spirit of our ancestors
whose stories continues…*

# Table of Contents

Reflexive Energy ...................................................... 1

Dimensions of Music ................................................ 3

The Body ................................................................ 23

Dance No More ..................................................... 29

It's All Relative ....................................................... 35

Meet the Authors ................................................... 45
    Glenn L. McDonald ..................................................... 46
    Terri E. Lyons ............................................................... 47
    L.T. Woody ................................................................... 48
    Mario D. King ............................................................... 49
    RYCJ ............................................................................. 50

Thank You .............................................................. 51

More Books ............................................................ 52

Glenn McDonald

# Reflexive Energy

LET'S TALK about energy. Not in a geopolitical, fossil fuel vs. solar vs. wind type of way. Let's talk about human energy or rather the energy you have as a human. Most people realize in this world everything gives off energy, especially human beings. However, what many people may not realize is that your energy is reflexive. Meaning you get back what you put out or even more basically, we are mirrors to each other. "When you're smiling, the whole world smiles at you…" That's not just a song lyric. That is life. Others will mirror back the genuine energy you exude when interacting.

For instance, I recently was annoyed with a good friend of mine. We have known each other for a while and their tendencies started to grate on me. Rather than be the open and honest person I should have been and let them know about my annoyances, I chose to be indirect. This manifested itself in some times minor, sometimes major ways. I would make snide comments. Or I would make a situation more difficult than it needed to be. I would disagree for the sake of disagreement. This led to a further strained friendship.

Now looking back, I can see my energy had much to do with the deterioration of the relationship. Had I met the situation with understanding, openness and caring, it may have had a different outcome. I didn't see that my energy could turn the relationship trajectory around, which ended the relationship. All the negativity killed it.

## Reflexive Energy

From this experience I learned I had the power to turn around the relationships in my life. I started to try and act in a way that I wanted others to act. Another friend of mine had a similar issue. However, they told me (and I thought it was crazy at the time) that they would solve it with positivity and love. I thought "this is insane" and prepared my popcorn and soda for the fireworks of this inevitable failure of a solution.

I watched as my friend and the "other" would have discussions. But instead of attacking or using snide comments as I had done with my antagonist, he would respond with kind words or understanding statements. "I understand" was a constant in their dialogues. Shockingly, their relationship improved. The problem friend would offer solutions when my friend would voice a concern that was encapsulated by an "I understand" statement. The judging went away and the problem friend, if you can even call him that at this point, met altercations with the same type of understanding.

This story is vital for this space because I believe compassion and understanding is missing from the world today, yet it is something we all crave. The more we can spread the word that our actions and energy is reflexive and will alter the energy of those around us, the more the world will be a fulfilling and satisfying place.

# Dimensions of Music

WE JUST FINISHED DINNER when dad got up from the table and went downstairs into the recreation room.

I had completed my homework and helped mother clear the table. I wanted to make sure there wasn't any reason why I couldn't watch *Laugh-In*.

The television had just warmed up when I heard the Hi-Fi playing a record from downstairs. I was torn between looking at the show and seeing what dad was doing. I decided to tip downstairs and find out what he was up to.

I saw my father sitting next to the Hi-Fi with music paper in his lap. He was playing the 45 version of Duke Ellington's *I've Got It Bad*.

Without saying a word I sat on the sofa across from him. I liked to watch him work and try to figure how he was able to make notes on the paper from the sounds he heard. He didn't see me at first.

Dad took the needle off the record and went to the piano. He played one key at first and then made a chord with several fingers. The chords sounded the same as the chords on the record. In complete silence he wrote each note onto his music paper. Then he looked up at me and smiled.

"Listen. Listen closely to the horns," he said. He put the needle back on the record. He explained the difference between the tenor sax playing the lyric and the alto and baritone playing the melody. He played the melody on the piano only this time he played what he had written. He put my hands on the piano and molded my fingers to the right keys. I played my first chord and it was the biggest thrill I ever had. I had forgotten all about *Laugh-In*.

He picked up his guitar and strummed a few chords. He tightened up the strings using his tuning fork.

"Try to find this on the piano," he instructed.

I struck a few keys and then hit the right one that was in tune with him. We did it three times. Then he told me to find the E note. He made the guitar whine somehow, but brought it right in tune with the piano. We ended up playing scales together. Then he listened as I played all by myself. He let me go at it for a while, but then he had to get back to work. I watched my father for the rest of the evening playing the record over and again, meticulously writing each note for first and second tenor, first and second alto, trumpet and baritone, what he called the reed section. Then he wrote the entire piece again for piano.

I went to bed that night with the song on my mind and woke up the next day, singing the lyrics all through school. From the start, I was different from most of my classmates. One of the differences was singing songs most of them never heard of.

Thursday evening was rehearsal night. I made sure my homework was complete so I could sit in the corner out of everyone's way and listen.

The musicians filed in the front door and went downstairs with mom, full of lively talk and laughter.

The drummer came in through the back door with loads of duffle bags and drums. As the drummer was setting up, the sax man, Mister Joe, put his horn together. Mister James doodled on his trumpet. Dad plugged in the amps and the bass man, Mister ray, almost shook the house tuning it up. The piano man, Mister Stan, was the last one to arrive. He took his seat at the piano playing for pleasure. Nobody was playing anything in particular. It was just a lot of noise. But there was something about the sound of any instrument that brought excitement into the house. The bandstands were set with a music book on each one. Mom brought ice-cold Ballentine beer for each of the guys.

Dad had the guys quiet down and talked about what was on the agenda for the night and the upcoming affair on Saturday. They began playing a tune I heard many times before; Bill Doggett's *Honky Tonk*. Dad started off playing the first eight bars. I know because I counted them. Then all of the sax men came in. Finally, Mister Joe did a solo.

I couldn't keep still. Mister Joe ground out gritty sounds while Mister Ray hit the bottom on his bass and walked it to the top. I saw shadows of feet standing near the jalousie window. Our neighbors were on our patio dancing and finger popping. By the end of the song the band members were confident of their performance and the people on the patio gave applause. Beer cans were popping as dad lead them into the arrangement he just completed the night before. He started from the bridge.

Everyone was quiet as dad counted. He only wanted the melody. Dad provided the rhythm and first and second alto began on the count of four. I not only remembered

Dimensions of Music

each chord they played, I understood it. I saw the image in my mind, how dad molded my hands to the keys to make the sound. I understood the discipline and cooperation necessary to make the sound perfect and powerful. They played the bridge two more times and the third time my mother sang the lyric.

"Now when the week is all over…"

She sang as delicate inflections from the reed moved my spirit along with them. It was smooth and mellow. Just as I was getting into it, Dad stopped the music. He wanted the drummer and baritone to come in.

Starting from the bridge once more, the full sound was vibrant and clear. It sent chills all through me. Each musician enriched the sound of the other. Mom came in. It was as if the band picked her up and carried her on a melodic journey with them.

"And Friday rolls around…"

She closed her eyes as she exaggerated the lyric with soul or perhaps pain. Whatever it was, I was mesmerized. Mister Joe stood up to do his thing and blew my head off at the same time.

Fine beads of sweat made his forehead glow. His eyes closed tightly, almost painfully when without missing a beat and took it home.

"Oh, now he don't love, like I love him…

but a… nobody could…"

The rec room glowed with smiles and laughter after the end.

Dad wasn't overly emotional, at least not most the time. He nodded his head and looked at mom and that was enough for both of us. The pride that goes along with a profound sense of accomplishment was evident from the musicians and onlookers alike. I was particularly proud because they were my parents who created the incredible moment we had that night. It was the power of music.

𝄞 ♭ ¢

Saturday night and it was time to get ready for the big affair.

*The Kappas, Rho Chapter* were having the annual *Harvest Moon Ball* at the *Sheraton Hotel* in Philadelphia. While dad loaded the car with his microphones, column speakers and amps, mom was upstairs applying make-up, eyelashes and squeezing into her beautiful gown. I helped zip her dress and watched her apply touches of glamour. I was so excited because I was going too. It was my first time to see them on stage in front of approximately three thousand guests.

Mom made me comfortable at *table one* where I could see everything and was safely out of the way. As dad was setting up I walked onto the huge stage. I looked up at the lights of every color that seemed to be pointed in every direction. The musicians arrived in tuxedos. I looked at the ballroom floor. Tables were numbered and dressed in fine linen complete with a candle and glasses. The tables surrounded a huge dance floor under dimly lit chandeliers. The ladies were dressed in beautiful flowing gowns. Delightful perfume gently filled the air as they entered. I turned my attention back to dad. He was set up, almost ready to begin. The guys in the band had taken their place and were tuning up. Dad plugged in his cassette player and then walked toward me. He said he was ready to do a sound check and took me with him.

We walked upstairs onto the balcony. The chandeliers were huge and the people, still filing in, were amusingly small. Dad and I leaned over the ionic marble banister listening to my favorite song; *Aquarius, Let the Sunshine In.'* I wanted to dance, but dad wanted me to pay attention to the quality of the sound. The bass, he said, was fine but the treble was a little too low.

"When the treble is too low, the sound is muddled. The singers don't come through as crisp as they should," dad said.

I didn't understand what he meant until we came back to the stage and he made adjustments on his amplifier. It seemed like magic to me how the timbre of the entire song changed with just the turn of a few knobs.

The crowd settled in. They were table-hopping amid soft laughter and ice clicking in the glasses. Mom, buried in the crowd with hugs from guests, I heard her laughing as she made her way to our table, *table one*. There was a coke with a fruit salad on top just for me.

I looked onto the stage at the ten-piece band. They were looking sharp in their tuxedos. The brass sparkled under the stage lights. Dad stood tall with his polished Jaguar Fender shining. He turned to face the band.

"Heads Up," he said in an almost military fashion.

I heard him direct the band by calling a number. That number corresponded to the song in their arrangement book he was ready to play. The band began to play, *'Something.'*

All of the beautiful ladies and gentlemen filled the floor dancing to my father's music. They were beautiful. I watched their elegance and grace as they swept across from one end to the other. I wanted to be just like them. My mother came and sat beside me after greeting almost everyone there. She made sure I was okay and then went to take her place on stage.

The intro had big-band fanfare. I followed every note they played. I remembered the work and some of the arguments in effort to make it right. I remembered mom learning the lyrics and singing while preparing dinner. All of their work, their sweat, frustration and arguing paid off. That night, the song took the audience into a melodic escapade of romance.

The spot was right on mom. Her black sequin gown changed colors under the lights. The audience greeted her with vibrant applause and then she began to sing.

'Something in the way he moves…attract me like no other lover…'

I was filled with romance, almost falling in love with everyone there. All of the ladies were gorgeous and elegantly dressed and all of the men were handsome. They held each other close. The riffs from the reed enriched the mood. I was proud of them and optimistic about my

Dimensions of Music

future because I knew the talent and discipline they had was inside of me as well.

My favorite part was coming up. Fast music. I knew it because Mister Joe stood up. He hit the first note I remembered from the record *'Tune-up'*. He didn't play it exactly like Junior Walker. He played it his way. It didn't take long before the guests Bopped all over the floor.

Laughs, smiles and sometimes a scream got the night going. The party was on. Mom came on again and kept the crowd going with *'In the Midnight Hour.'* The piano man, Mister Stan had mama's back as he stomped on the keys.

The gift of music is incredible. It can bring a tear, excite romance, or throw a crowd into a wild charade of dance and laughter. I was smiling as the crowd carried on. The elegant gowns at the beginning of the evening were shaking and jumping by now. Some had even taken their evening sequin shoes off to slide all over the floor. One of the men came over to me and took my hand. I looked at mom. She was still singing and nodded her head to me at the same time. I got on the floor and danced my heart out. I knew the breaks. I knew when they were going to the bridge and when they took it home. Nothing else mattered. The night belonged to them and to me.

After intermission mom returned to the stage to sing *'I've Got it Bad.'* The synchrony of the tenor sax and the sweet solo of the trumpet were like a full body massage. I wasn't old enough to have a drink or experience the influence of hormones or romantic love, but from the eyes of a child it was easy to see how people can fall in love and dance the night away.

𝄞 ♭ ¢

Mom and dad had some friends over on Saturday night. They pushed all of the furniture out of the way and the kitchen was filled with all kinds of Saturday night party food. They were laughing and talking up a storm. The Hi-Fi was set with records that kept the living room ablaze with dance and song. Booker T's *'Green Onions'* came on. I watched as they began to do a dance called *'the Madison'* in the middle of the floor. It didn't even matter when the song was over. They kept the beat going until the next record played; *'Stubborn Kinda Fellow.'*

Later, they decided to have a little jam session. I sat on the steps and watched dad get his guitar. One of the guests, Mister Morris, took a seat at the piano. He began to play a Ray Charles tune, *'Let's Go Get Stoned'*. He and mom sang it together while dad provided a little rhythm. Mister Morris hit those bottom keys as he sang, *'Ain't no harm, to have a little taste…'*

And then mom sang, 'But don't loose your cool and start messin' up the man's place…'

Then he sang, 'Ain't no harm, to take a little nip…'

Then mom sang, 'but don't you fall down and bust your lip?'

Then everybody sang and sent chills up and down my spine? *'Let's go get stoned!'*

Dimensions of Music

The more liquor they drank, the louder they played. My dad didn't drink, but the rest of them made up for him. Mister Morris said he wanted to do a little Louis Jordan. He began to play *'Is you is, or is you ain't my baby?'*

I knew the words to that one and I began to sing it right along with them. I got so carried away I came down the steps popping my finger and singing the song like I was grown. They welcomed me into their party for a minute. When the song was over mom gave me a look. It was all I needed to see for me to get back upstairs.

𝄞 ♭ ¢

Mom was going through the cedar closet and found her old 78's. She told me these were the only kind of records that existed when she was a young girl. Some of the big artists from that time were Anita O'Day, Ella Fitzgerald, and Illinois Jacquet among many others.

One of her favorites was Billie Holiday. Mom went through the records and pulled up, *'The Very Thought of You.'* She told me to turn on the Hi-Fi and let it warm up.

Mom flipped the needle so the 78 could play. The song began with the piano. It was light and lyrical. There wasn't much tenor or bass to the sound, but it was clear.

I heard Billie's voice for the first time. It was initially strange. I'd never heard a voice like that. It was haunting, yet inviting. Mom sang every word and made Billie come alive for me. She enjoyed it so much that soon I began to enjoy it too. I asked her to play it again. This time I knew at least some of the words and we sang it together. We sang our hearts out.

'The very thought of you...and I forget to do...Those little ordinary things... that everyone ought to do...'

That's when I fell in love with Billie Holiday. I fell in love with her soul and her pain. Mom brought it to me. I felt the power once again of music. Mom made the soul of every vocalist come to life. The Ink Spots composed a song titled *'Whispering Grass.'* It was the most delightful explanation about trouble gossip can bring. She taught me the lyric and the wisdom behind it. She told me that music addresses every occasion in life if you let it.

I found myself taking songs apart just like I heard dad do. Listening to Billie Holiday, I also listened to Lester Young's full sound on tenor saxophone and knew his 'signature.' I listened to Teddy Wilson on piano and learned his signature as well. I could listen to a record and hear something different every time. All the artists I heard had their own sound. There was never any mistake as to who they were. There wasn't any imitation. They had their voice and they sang or played their story.

𝄞 ♭ ¢

**E**very **G**ood **B**oy **D**oes **F**ind for my right hand and **F.A.C.E.** for my left.

Dad made sure I positioned my hands with my palms up and gave me exercises to do before I began each lesson. I had been attending Warner Brothers Piano Studio for only a few months, but I felt like a maestro. I was learning to play Beethoven's Ninth but really wanted to play some of the funky music dad and his crew played

Dimensions of Music

every Thursday night. The music book was straight and correct, but after a while it became a little boring. Without thinking about it I found myself doing small improvisations on any tune I was learning to play. Dad warned me however, of the importance of learning and developing technique within confines of the metronome. Then I can play it anyway I want to. One hour each day I perfected technique. The second hour I created.

$\S \; \flat \; ¢$

Dad brought a huge black box into the house. He needed mom's help to help him get it in. He rolled it into the rec room and took the vinyl cover off. I didn't know what to make of it. He brought out his guitar and all the plugs and wires that went along with it and connected it to this black box. He turned the power on and a huge hmm vibrated throughout the room. Then he whipped out a pedal and began to strike a few chords. It sounded just like the music from the movie *Shaft*!

The big box, he said, is called a Leslie. He had it custom made from a music store. It was capable of making his guitar sound like anything he wanted; an echo, an organ, a harp, anything. It was great. I watched him fiddle with the controls and create beautiful sounds. Some were a little strange, but fascinating. The pedal, he told me, was called a Cry Baby, a *wawa* pedal. The he began to play the theme from *Shaft*. He bought the 45 record and listened and wrote. He practiced and listened and practiced more. He sat in silence and wrote.

Thursday night rehearsal and all of the guys were amazed at this new Leslie. They were also excited about practicing the hot new song. They'd already been playing on their own. So they started by breaking the tune apart.

With no rhythm, the reed section just blew their part. They tapped their foot to keep time. Silence between the notes embodied the discipline and concentration. Each musician played his piece individually and then they all played together.

Next, it was just the drummer expressing the unique percussive beat heard at the beginning of the piece. He kept it up for some time and then dad came in with his guitar featuring his *wawa* pedal. The two of them beat it out.

Bass man, Mister Ray played his part. It was guitar, bass and drums. They kept it working for about half an hour. Then they took a break. Mom had the Ballentine ice-cold and they talked about who had seen the movie and the social changes that made such a movie possible.

After the break I heard dad say, "Okay fellas, let's take it from the top."

Drummer man started off in his percussive fury again. Then dad worked his *wawa*. Mister Ray came in and the reed flowed. Mom brought up the rear with her tambourine. It all came together. I saw feet on the patio through the window and went upstairs to the front door. My friends and neighbors were sitting and standing all over finger popping. Then all at once they sang *Shaft*! I'm sure mom and dad's Saturday affair was a blast, but I also know it couldn't beat the delight felt throughout the house that night. I stayed outside with my friends and neighbors, peeking through the window along with them. Mom grabbed the microphone. Everyone quieted down in anticipation of what they were going to play next.

Mom began to sing…

'Cold…Now I can't believe your heart is cold…'

There was silence.

'Maybe slow to warm from a long lonely night…'

The drummer beat up the fanfare. Guitar and bass came in right on cue as mom did her rendition of *'Watch What Happens.'* A couple of neighbors began to Bop right on our patio! Mama was swinging that song. The lyrics rolled from her with style and comfort that gave a laid back groove everyone enjoyed.

She came off the bridge…

'Oh, how now won't you let somebody…with a deep love to give… Give that deep love to you…and what magic you'll see…'

I heard the flat and sharp notes enhancing every other measure as they brought it home. Mom soon joined the party on the piano. It put everyone in a good mood; the way friends and neighbors should be. A few people brought cool drinks and another neighbor treated all the kids to Good Humor ice-cream.

And then…

I don't know what dad did to make his guitar have the wild crazy sound he needed to play *Scorpio*. Mister Ray, the bass player had a long solo that sent everyone absolutely nuts. It was a bigger deal than I imagined. Cars were slowing down and some people pulled to the side and looked up from the sidewalk. Mister Ray was still getting down and the guys were imitating playing bass. Dad took it home with his sound showing off his skills. Applause and screams now filled the street, the patio and my home. It was one hell of a night.

𝄞 ♭ ¢

The band was rehearsing something I never heard before. It had a nice beat, but it sounded... well, foreign.

Indeed it was. Mom explained to me that they were hired to do a Jewish wedding. They were playing *Hava Nagila*. It's a song that is part of the Jewish tradition celebrating the newlywed couple. Mom told me everyone joins in and it was a lovely dance to see. She further discussed with me the importance of music as a function of exposure. She encouraged me not to just listen to the music I hear on the radio, but to stretch my horizon in the language of music...to relish an auditory nutrition for my spirit... to raise my consciousness of other cultures.

Waltzes were corny to me. I saw people waltzing in old *Bette Davis* movies. I thought it was music only fitting for rich white people from long ago.

Then one night I went with mom and dad for the *South Jersey Debutante Ball*. The young ladies dressed in formal white partnered with their young tuxedoed men. They gradually waltzed across the floor at the *Atlantic City Convention Center*. It wasn't corny anymore. The waltz was like a courtship. They formally greeted one another and

## Dimensions of Music

took each other by hand. The ladies curtsied in synchrony causing their gowns to go into full bloom across the floor.

I saw the same beauty when dad performed for the *Hess's of Allentown Fashion Show* at the *Ben Franklin Hotel*. Nothing was more fitting than waltzing on a spring afternoon watching stunning models gracefully saunter down the runway. They moved as fluently as the music showcasing fine fabric and delicate details of fashion that most people in the audience could never afford.

$ ♭ ¢

A maternal cousin of mine passed away and my parents and I were on our way to church. The Pipe organ hummed as we walked the aisle to view the body and give condolences to the immediate family.

A lady from the choir stood up and walked to the microphone to sing *Let My Work Speak For Me*.

When she began to sing, the moment was reverent. There were a few *Amens* and muddled whimpers in the congregation, but that was about it. Then she sang the second verse with southern old school soul. The organist rocked the church as the entire congregation joined in and sang *Let My Work Speak For Me*. People stood up and tears were streaming. I didn't realize my face was wet too. Even those who remained seated were rocking back and forth. It was not possible to sit still. I had been to church service and heard many soul stirring hymns, but this was the first time I felt a hymn touch the core of my soul. Perhaps it was the Holy Spirit touching me, but no doubt it was the music that made it undeniably real.

Let My Work Speak For Me.

𝄞 ♭ ₵

My parents and I were on our way to the *Latin Casino*. After dinner the Emcee welcomed the audience to the show. The opening group was *'The Mighty Clouds of Joy,'* but the main attraction was Al Green.

Throughout the night dad and I exchanged looks as we connected to Al Green's reed section and soulful sounds that played. His band was arranged the same as dad's; trumpets in front, alto sax to the right, and tenor toward the left. Al Green's hit *'Here I Am Baby'*, has detailed riffs throughout. Dad and I played with our fingers catching it all. He made slow horizontal gestures with his fingers when they held a note and then rocked his head catching each break. Mom sang right along with Al. We had our own concert in the middle of the feature show.

𝄞 ♭ ₵

Every time I listen to the radio or play a record, I take the song apart. *Chicago* and *The Average White Band* were the best groups to dissect. I listened to the blend of the reed or the staccato riff at the bridge. Then I'd shift my listening to the rhythm, especially if the bass hits the bottom and walks to the top. The lingering plea from a sax or trumpet places me in an orbit to appreciate the story behind the musician.

I still remember the labels from almost every record mom and dad had. Long before I could read I learned to remember the color and emblem of each label and was

Dimensions of Music

---

able to find the record they were looking for faster than they could. They were amazed how I was able to find them so quickly. They didn't understand how I was able to do it and at the time I wasn't old enough to explain it. It's a good system and it still works. It carried over to dad's album collection. I became fixated on artwork of the jackets and associated each with the artist. The art was an appetizer to the main entrée of the album. Some seemed to portray a voyeuristic view into the soul of the person behind the music. Shadow, silhouettes, the sweat on a wine bottle at sunset; the somber face of Ray Charles under a blue light increased my desire to listen to their stories.

𝄞 ♭ ¢

There's nothing like a day in New York to see the Broadway Show *'The Wiz'* starring Stephanie Mills. After a lovely dinner my parents and I took our seats waiting for the show to begin. A huge applause echoed throughout the theater when the light dimmed. There was nothing to see at the onset of the prologue—at first.

Slowly the orchestra rose from the floor as the theater swelled, symphonic sounds of every instrument known to man filling the theater. The lights reacted to the music and it seemed every note came inside of me. It was right in front of me, behind me, beside me, and on top of my head at the same time. They did a medley of every song for the play. I was mesmerized and thought I'd heard it all when Stephanie sang *As Soon As I Get Home*.

But no, she had a crowd crazy with love for her when she sang *If You Believe*. A big rich beautiful voice flowed out of this petite lady with perfect acoustic from the orchestra. I had never heard anything like it before. Tears came from my eyes as she carried the crowd into pure euphoria in her plead to just believe in yourself. When she looked upon where I was sitting, it was as if she was singing to me—just me. She pleaded once more to me to believe in myself. She lifted her tiny arms in her cute little dress and once again sang...

'If you believe in yourself...Just believe in yourself... as I believe in you...'

Talk about influence.

𝄞 ♭ ¢

The coalescence of melody and lyric has the ability to define and address a range of humanity that for me, no other art form can do. As music changed over the years, I still cling to the music from my youth. I find solace in the music my parents introduced to me.

The muted trumpet of Miles Davis speaks to the little girl that is always alone. The pop and bounce of Count Basie beckons me to jump right along with him. The romance only Johnny Hodges created with the Duke Ellington band still makes a sultry night complete and peaceful. The unmistakable aria of Benny Goodman feels like a soothing hot bubble bath. I carry music with me. I recite poetry to music. I dance while preparing a meal. I reflect on a song as I cry. I listen to music to heal. I shout a song in joy and praise. I recite a lyric for strength. I remember a lyric when faced with ugly life. When I'm sitting in silence or when I find myself somewhere I'd

## Dimensions of Music

rather not be, I always have my favorite melodies in my head to carry me through the day.

How can one live without music in their soul?

## The Body

MAN, I DONE had some weird times in my life you know. I mean, in my fourteen years on this planet, I have lived enough for ten people. Some of the things I've done would make your hair stand on end, but the only bad thing about it is that everything that happens to me is something I don't want to happen. The good things in life like a good piece of cake, or no school, or seein' something that has been run over by a truck never happen to me.

Now take the summer, about five years ago when me, and the rest of my family went down south to the country for my grandmother's funeral. To tell the truth, the only ones goin' for a funeral was my mother and father, 'cause me and my little brother was just goin' down there to miss the last few days of school and chase them country girls and whatnot. I remember thinking that finally it looked like my luck had changed.

The ride down there to North Carolina was a long one, and I don't really remember much about it 'cause we were asleep most of the time. That is, until we woke up after the car hit a big bump in the road, which turned out to be a rabbit whose leg we had run over. My dad and his brother got out to take a look at the poor thing and decided to bring it into the car since it was still alive. This was good, because they gave it to me to hold onto and it gave my brother and me something to do for a while. We wrapped it in a blanket and just kept rubbing its soft fur. It reminded me of a rabbit I used to take care of in my first grade class. I remember how one day I came to school

# The Body

and the janitor told me the rabbit had died, so he had thrown it out. I thought that was kinda' cold.

Well anyway, we got down there and there were all my uncles and aunts cryin' all over the place, faintin' and pissin' on themselves 'cause their mother had died. Me and my brother figured they must have just lost their minds. I mean, I guess people dyin' didn't mean much to us then, especially when we didn't really know the person. I had only seen my grandmother once and my brother had never seen her. So, all of this was like a big joke to my brother and me. We didn't do nothin' but run around the coffin (which for some reason I couldn't understand, was inside the house in the living room), look at the body, watchin' people faint and stuff like that.

There was one thing that happened that sort of' messed things up some. Me and my brother went out onto the porch and ran into my grandfather. He was this kinda' short, toothless, scary looking guy with all this gray hair all over his face and everything, and he had this big bloody knife in his hand. He was sittin' on a wooden stool with a steel washtub in front of him and the bucket had all this blood and fur in it. When he saw us walk up, he smiled and held up this pink and red animal carcass for us to look at -- that he had just finished skinning!

"This here rabbit you brought us should make some good eatin' for our supper this evenin', and we is mighty grateful to you," he said softly.

At this, my brother's eyes got all big and round and he screamed, then right away he ran back into the house wavin' his arms and yellin' his head off, which nobody paid much attention to since that sorta' thing was going on all day anyway.

All I could do was stand there looking at that bloody rabbit with his skin all pulled off, remembering how soft his fur felt as I rubbed it in the back seat of the car. So, I didn't eat much for supper that night. These country folk were strange I could see, 'cause they sure did enjoy that rabbit.

Other than that, we were still havin' a real good time and it looked like things were about to get even better when some of our country cousins came over. That is, until all of us were out there sittin' on the porch and they started tellin' them ghost stories. Man, they was tellin' us about how ghosts, monsters, and stuff came out of dead people that you keep in a house for too long. Me and my brother was so dumb that we just took in every word they said, and after they were through scarin' us and had gone home, we were too afraid to set foot in that house again. However, all of a sudden, we kept hearin' these monsters under the porch or maybe it was on the roof, but anyway we ran inside before it got us – whatever it was.

As soon as we stepped in the door, our mother told us to go upstairs to bed. I stared back at her kinda' funny 'because I knew she had to be crazy. She thought we was goin' to go up them dark stairs where all them monsters and stuff was while that dead body was sittin' in the living room.

Shucks! The woman was definitely deranged, she was a sick person and her kind needs to get some help.

# The Body

Man, suppose one of them monsters got after us. It was gonna' be too far to jump out of the window and if we ran down the stairs, we had to run right past the daggone body. Anyways, after we argued for about an hour, my mom said that she had had enough and she pulled out what we called 'the whip', and when the whip comes out you go and we went, and we went fast – so fast. In one second we were up the stairs, took off all of our clothes, closed the windows, pulled down the shades, hopped into bed, pulled the covers and pillows over our heads and after about ten minutes, we noticed something was not right.

"Hey man, you left the lights on," I whispered.

"Naw man, you the oldest, you supposed to turn the lights off," he whispered back.

"Naw man, Mama said the youngest is supposed to turn off the lights so he can catch up to the number of times I did it while you was little."

My brother is dumb so he leaped out of the bed and ran to turn the lights off and when he tried to get back into bed, I would not let him in. So of course, he started kickin' and screaming about how the monsters was chewin' up his leg and they were pullin' him away and stuff like that, so I let him get back into bed – and that's when we heard it.

There were these footsteps at the bottom of the stairs and they were heavy footsteps, like bodies have. They were comin' up the stairs, and me and my brother was so scared that we got all wrapped up in the covers and moved to the far side of the bed.

We could hear these feet hittin' each step really hard and slow like it was tryin' hard to make us hear it and, you know, to scare us more. By now, my brother was cryin' his heart out, but I told him he had to cry real quiet so the monster wouldn't know where we was.

"Shut up, man! You gonna make the body know where we at, and if it finds out, I'm gonna push your butt out so that it can eat you up 'cause you know I never really liked you no way," I whispered.

We could hear the steps creak as the body neared the top of the stairs and we was both shakin' real bad, and now the bed was wet 'cause my brother couldn't control himself. The body was at the top of the stairs now and that's when we just started screamin' at the top of our lungs, and that was the exact wrong thing to do 'cause that made it run real fast over to the bed. So, when it grabbed us, we jumped off the other side of the bed and crawled under it. We didn't notice at the time but the body was screamin' too, but we didn't hear nothin' 'cause we was way too scared.

All of a sudden it grabbed our legs and started pullin' on us and we were holdin' onto the legs of the bed, but it yanked us loose so we tried to grab onto the floor, but it pulled us out anyway so we just gave up 'cause it had us. As we lay there all tangled up in our blanket, we heard it walk over and turn on the lights, and there she was, Mama – and in her hand was…the whip!

## Dance No More

AS THE SUN pierced thru the cracks of the closed blinds, Elijah was awakened by the sweet smell of hickory-smoked bacon. With excitement he jumped out bed as this only meant one thing—Jamma and Paw-Paw were visiting. Stumbling over cords to his video game he dashed past the wall decorated with his favorite players from the National Basketball Association and approached his bedroom door grabbing a pair of rolled up socks from the laundry basket sitting atop his dresser. He proceeded to toss them towards the plastic hoop wedged between the doorframe and his bedroom door. With a cracking voice produced by puberty he whispered, "Elijah for three…"

The subtlest of pastel and creams was within view as Elijah entered the kitchen. With the corners of his mouth showing the aftermath of a good night's sleep, Elijah was about to mutter his arrival. A small woman in stature with skin as dark and smooth as the night's sky had a face of delight as she said, "One day mong all. Mawnin chil'."

"Good Morning Jamma. Good Morning Ma." Elijah replied.

"Rest you mouth. Come'yuh an gi' me hug," Jamma replied in her strong Geechee accent. While slightly shaking her head with the giggles she continued, "Milk ain't dry off e mouf yet."

Jamma laughed with Elijah's mother as they set the table. Elijah was always amused when his grandmother spoke in her native tongue. With a hand quicker than the

# Dance No More

speed of sound he was able to grab a piece of that sweet smelling bacon before the brown side of his hand was met with a wooden spoon.

"Where is Paw-Paw?" Elijah asked as he scarfed down the last remnants of his favorite breakfast delight. The brown sugar that Jamma lightly coated the bacon with always caused his taste buds to dance.

Dance taste buds—dance.

Shooing Elijah away from the bacon, his mother replied. "He's in the den with his eyes glued to the television with your father." As she began to pour some warm grits in a bowl she said, "tell both of them it's time to eat their breakfast."

Elijah nodded as he tried to make another move for some bacon, but this time he was met with double resistance by the two strong women preparing the meal. At that point he knew he was defeated.

"What's up Paw-Paw," Elijah stated as he entered the den. He noticed that the room was more somber than it had been in the kitchen.

"Hey there Rocket," his grandfather replied.

Elijah looked towards his dad and saw that he was deeply immersed with the television. He barely knew Elijah had made his presence.

Elijah whispered to his grandfather, "What are y'all watching?"

His grandfather slightly shook his head and replied. "We're watching a story I never thought we would still be seeing after all these years later."

Now in tune with the conversation, Elijah's father signaled for his son to sit next to him. His face was glowering as he said, "son we're watching the aftermath of terrorism at its finest."

Elijah sat on the arm of the couch as he noticed that the act of terrorism happened in the hometown of his grandparents—Charleston, South Carolina.

Elijah's face became grave. "What happened?" Elijah asked. "How did he do that in a church?"

His father replied. "Hatred has no limits."

"What does that mean?" Elijah asked.

With sadden eyes, Paw-Paw looked in the direction of Elijah and said, "Rocket, what your father is telling you is that there are certain people in this here world who has a hatred so deep within them...that they are willing to go to all lengths to justify it."

Elijah tried to decode that message within his 13-year-old brain. He understood that there were issues beyond his dreams of becoming the next Steph Curry. His father always instilled within him a sense of awareness as it related to his culture and community.

"The world is like a spinning record...all coming full circle. I was no more than your age when I heard about those 4 little girls in Alabama," Paw-Paw said.

## Dance No More

Remembering the documentary he watched with his father about those 4 little girls, Elijah asked, "that was in a church too—right?"

Elijah's grandfather nodded. "And I can tell ya. That burned something inside of me that took me years to get over. That's when I became active."

A look of curiosity graced Elijah's face. "Active?"

"Yes, that's when to the disapproval of my parents—decided I was going to begin protesting and such. There was a case going on round that time in South Carolina. I think it was...uhm...I think it was Briggs—Briggs versus Elliot. You had people like Thurmond—Strom Thurmond that wanted to keep people of color in a certain place. But I wasn't gonna stand for it—not no more. I began participating in the Charleston Movement. People called it the emergence of the Charleston Negro. We stood for building and sustaining our own." Paw-Paw became sullen as he continued. "Have mercy Father."

Elijah's father's strong black hands gently griped Paw-Paw's shoulder as he sighed. "It's okay Pop. Don't let it get you all worked up. I'm worked up for the both of us. It's not your fight no more."

"You're wrong son." Paw-Paw replied. "It's my fight until I have no more fight left—and that's the day I shall be buried. I would be doing a disservice to those who marched and fought with me. The beatings and disrespect towards people of color plays like the song that never ends. So...when you say it's not my fight no more, you're right. It's not my fight—it's our fight."

Elijah sat expressionless.

Elijah's father sighed again as he began to pace the den. He began to think about his life. He began to think about its purpose. One word continued to cloud his mind. That word was — active. When his father said he got active, at that moment he realized that he could do more. He realized that it wasn't enough to just tell his son what to do and how to do it...he had to be active.

A voice that sounded like it came from miles away could be heard yelling. "Come and eat!"

Elijah remained with a fixed look upon his face. He began to think about all of the young black boys that lost their lives due to both police and neighborhood violence. That sweet smell of hickory-smoked bacon wasn't so sweet anymore. He no longer was in a mood to make his taste buds dance. Dance no more taste buds. Dance no more. There was a new taste bud arising within him and that taste was—justice.

# It's All Relative

WE DIDN'T KNOW any better. To us the world sounded, and certainly looked, like a pretty big place with a lot of unrelated people in it.

Up and down our block, the whole stretch of it connected to three other blocks, included twenty some odd houses, on either side, and not a one of those houses had a single known relative living in it.

Count it, as I just did. Roughly 188 houses and only one out of the 188 houses had people living in it related to me.

Of course we weren't paying it no never-mind when holidays like Thanksgiving rolled around and two 8-foot tables would be pushed together so that the heads of the family could eat at one table while the kids and junior heads of the family made use of little card-tables, the sofa and coffee tables, and the basement to enjoy our turkey dinners on.

Yeah, our family was that big, though we didn't know it. By extension we blindly enjoyed counting the number of kids each of grandparent had; nine siblings born to each grandparent on both sides.

Grandmom and grandpop, my father's parents had nine children, not counting three who died; two of the three stillborn. And Grandpop's mother Anna had 17 grand, which the rumor at first was his one sister had all those kids. Later the rumor was clarified, saying that Anna, who lived to 106, was counting the kids born to both her children. In other words, Grandpop's sister only had 8 or 9 kids, the last child, so it's been said, died with her, between her legs.

Now Madie and LC, and this is on my mother's side, they had big group too; nine, same number as my father's parents. Ironically, *so I always thought,* three also were stillborn, or died early. All that said, the family was gigantic, though in relation to the size of the world and the fact none of them lived on our block, even counting the trickle down effect of cousins born to our aunts and uncles didn't compute in our minds. A few hundred cousins didn't look like a whole lot when you only knew fifteen of them.

And then came one year when Madie came to our house to take us to Little Rock to spend the summer with her and our cousins.

All I remember was my mother telling us one day, like right out of a blue, that Madie was taking us *with her*. Next thing I knew we were at the airport. The Philadelphia International Airport. It was the second time we'd flown. The first time I don't recall much. Of that experience all I remember was hearing my mother's shrill piercing scream one night, and then being told we would have to miss school for a week. Vaguely I recall the hustle and bustle it took to orchestrate getting us all out of school, but then, just like what happens in a dream, one day I woke up standing in Madie's small home wrapped around my mother's leg, fearing an uncle who kept threatening to *get me*. He said he didn't care if I was wrapped around my mother's leg. He was still going to get me. Later I recall a lot of hollering and screaming; my aunts and uncles dealing with what I learned was my grandfather's death, but that was about as much of this trip I retained. I don't even remember how we got home, back up to Philly…unlike what came to be the case with the second trip we took to Little Rock.

We flew on the prestigious TWA. That I'll never forget. My aunt Lo, one of the middle daughters was a flight attendant for TWA. She was the highlight of the family on my mother's side. Yep, she was one of the first black flight attendants working for a major airline.

It was hot as all get out the day we left Philly for Little Rock to spend the summer. Dressed in what qualified as Sunday clothes; my sister and I dressed in soft cotton pastel colored dresses and my brother donned a miniature bowtie to go with his little soft Seersucker suit. My prima donna grandmother too, the absolute queen consistently upstaging gorgeous wasn't slacking in dress and style either. Dressed sharp as she wanted to be, she wore a classy pinkish pantsuit, had a jazzy chiffon scarf tied just beneath her chin, and worked up the whole beehive bun and had it sitting high up on her head. That, along with a pair of fashionable dark shades, the kind the Beetles and superstars wore, Madie had it going on! Didn't I say she was a queen? Well, she dressed the part too.

Later realized, we dressed this way because back in the day people were expected to dress like they had class when using services of similar class. Flying was high class, so we pulled out our good clothes to travel in style.

## It's All Relative

I still remember walking across the tarmac. Back then planes didn't pull up to the airport, but sat out in the open like the President of America's plane, for all watching from a large plate window to wave at us walking to the mountain of stairs that would put us on the plane. I looked back and waved up at my parents. They looked like Barbie and Ken dolls, albeit the chocolate set, standing so far back and high up. But I saw them waving too.

We hiked up what seemed like dozens of steps to board what even back then seemed like a small white jet with the TWA logo I loved staring at painted on the wing of the plane. There were two seats to a row of two lining either side of the plane inside. While I don't recall the seating arrangement, I vaguely recall another adult being with us. Maybe it was another aunt, I'm not sure, but the entire flight was without incident. The next memory I had of the trip was walking across another tarmac under a blistering hot sun. The muggy stifling air challenged the way I was used to breathing. I recall voicing my concern about the heat and someone *of adult stature* acknowledging my concern. We quickly were treated to water and right there in the airport I believe, were allowed to change into suitable attire. From then on, until the end of our stay in Little Rock, we dressed in summer clothes my mother packed.

But that was only the intro into our stay, as my next vivid memory was what I heard the moment I stepped foot in Madie's small house.

"Black gal! Come here black gal!"

That's how my mother's family in Little Rock talked, and when they used this phrase they usually were calling me.

I wasn't familiar with my father's family using such a phrase—ever. My northern family…parents, grandparents, aunts and uncles alike, would deliver a viral case of whoop-butt if they ever heard anyone referring to someone, especially in the family, by the term black. It was so much a taboo but it didn't bother me when I heard it used in Madie's house. I simply wasn't used to hearing "black" used this way. It almost sounded affectionate. In fact, I did take it in terms of endearment since so many of my mother's family were chocolate like me, and given the twang in the way they said it, along with the smiles on their faces. Whereas my father's family didn't speak like this, they were big on delivering *beat-downs*, and on tails of any size. My mother's family wasn't like that. They really were very sweet.

And even so, the phrase stuck because it was the interlude to something larger.

The attention inspired me to get loose and wild, and set myself free. Being raised in an environment that demanded respect *be shown*, and socially unfit traits *be suppressed*, it felt like the right place and a fine time to go buck wild.

On day uno, on the heels of that ceremonious eccentric greeting, our cousins showed us how they spelled *having fun*. We, about ten of us cousins, went out back behind Madie's house, a fairly big backyard where we—my siblings and I were introduced to a steep hill conjoined by

## It's All Relative

an abandoned lot. Dirt, rocks, sticks and stones jutting up from the dirt, and broken glass and other debris littered the hill and the lot.

We looked at each other, my sister, brother and I, expressing it all in our eyes when we were told we were going to slide down this hill.

*'No way,'* we may have even mouthed. There was at least a 15 to 20-foot drop, albeit at an incline. But to a 9, 8, and 6-year-old it might as well have been a drop from Mount Everest. These cousins are crazy was what I was thinking, and I'm sure my sister and brother were thinking much of the same.

But then one of our older cousins started calling for us to look around and find a box. A whole brown packing box mind you, which one of the cousins lo and behold did find.

The box was ripped open and the front and sides sort of rolled up to create a roller-coaster cart effect. It actually looked pretty inventive, so we indeed gave it a try. It was a scary ride down but a blast. Oh, how we all laughed and laughed at one of our older cousin's getting his toes and knuckles scraped and cut up sliding down that hill with us seated behind him. The ride was just like a makeshift rollercoaster, minus the health and safety controls that generally kept riders safe.

Later that day after we had what was called supper, we met what was called a family friend. Now, I don't recall the meal, but do recall many bragging about how Madie could make a whole meal out of a pinch of salt and a scoop of flower, like I recall the family friend who in all the years I'd never forgotten. He was an angel of a person who was called deaf and dumb; meaning, he couldn't hear or talk, prompting my curiosity to learn sign language, something we actually learned quite well over the summer.

Sleeping arrangements were quite interesting too. Madie's house (two bedrooms, one bathroom plus a small kitchen and living room all on one grand floor), made for a coziness different from our three-story, four-bedroom, one garage home that five people, not fifteen shared. My sister and I shared a room, but slept in separate beds. My brother had a room all to himself, and he had two beds—bunk beds.

But we weren't complaining. Again, this was all new to us, which surprisingly, for some strange reason the arrangement didn't seem so cramped. I hardly ever recall any fights over using the bathroom, though, it got pretty interesting learning how bathing was accomplished both inside as well as in the backyard.

At any rate, on to us not knowing any better, *and speaking of cousins and how small the world really is*. As our summer dwindled down to its end, after sliding down dirt hills in flattened cardboard boxes, eating whole tomatoes like fruit, save for salt sprinkled on top to act like a garnish, and enjoying a day at an amusement park on only a dollar where we somehow managed to ride every ride, including a Ferris Wheel where my country cousins tried to rock the cage off its cradle in attempt to get our monies worth, Madie one evening, tells us she's taking us to the country to meet some more of our cousins.

## It's All Relative

Again, what did we know? We thought we were already in the country, but come to find out, there is actually a country in the country.

Madie loaded all 10 of us on the back of her pick-up truck…red if I recall right, with a couple of aunts sitting up front in the cab with her, and *took off* for the country. No seat belts, no problem. As instructed we held on tight, sliding none-the-less around the bed of the truck as she careened over similar gravel we spent half the summer sliding down. Laughing and jumping around we were enjoying the time of our life, doing what we'd never done back home.

Every so often one of us, admittedly mostly me, would yell an obscenity for sure at a passerby where Madie or one of the aunts sitting up front would lean out the window, telling us to sit still. We would for a second, but then another second later would be back at it, jumping around, especially me, yelling the obscenities and insults at passersby.

"Stop it, y'all sit still," my aunts and Madie called out every so often from the cab.

But nooo, those instructions made no sense to the *black gal* high on this new lifestyle. Sitting still simply was no fun. Inconceivably, I knew nothing about Emmett Till. That event happened nearly two decades ago, even if I was the same innocent child only separated by time. To my good fortune, albeit however unknown, were the ancestral back roads Madie careened over, led foot to the pedal, kicking up dirt searing errant tree limbs in her path as we

42

continued hurling insults and debris we found on the floor of the truck at all objects, still and moving.

But on Madie sped on, fast too, bumping all of us around like *boomp, boomp, boomp* Chittty-Chitty Bang-Bang style, all of us sliding from one side of the truck to the other, laughing, having way too much fun, when suddenly Madie hit the brakes.

Screech! Just like that, with no warning at all, she came to a sudden, abrupt, unexpected stop. I got a little nervous then. I had just yelled something not so nice to these people she abruptly stopped in front of. I hoped it was a pit stop, like the pit stop she made a little prior to this stop. It wasn't uncommon for her to see a store sitting far back off the road and she barrel on for it to pick up some catfish. She did that once too, except it wasn't this time. This time she stopped in front of these people who just stood in front of us kind of looking at us… fingers twiddling in the ears sort of like, staring like we were the ones coming out of the cornfields.

"Meet y'all cousins," Madie said hopping out of the truck.

Gulp. But then like I said: what did we know? Or what did I know was more like it? To me the world sounded like a pretty big place, and certainly looked like a big place with a lot of unrelated people in it. How would I have known all these people were our cousins too?

Of course the obvious lesson is to treat others the way you want to be treated, yet the nobler lesson is it's a small world, as in…*it's all relative.*

# Meet the Authors

## Glenn L. McDonald

Glenn is an emerging screenwriter and accomplished video producer at the Foreign Service Institute. He directed the award-winning short film SHORT DAYDREAMS, which won honors at the Washington DC 24-Hour Film Festival. He also blogs and is a Multimedia Specialist for pop culture movie site FilmFad.com and is consultant for OSAAT Entertainment. Glenn's other passions are working out, practicing yoga or meditating when not writing or watching a movie to review. Glenn resides in Arlington, Virginia.

## Terri E. Lyons

Native of Philadelphia, Pennsylvania and a graduate of Harcum College Terri was the recipient of the *Best Storytellas in Town* contest, and is a spoken word artist, public speaker and the author of several memoirs, poetry books, and the debut novel Puzzles. Research, history, music, and performing original poetry at open mics and local cafés is her passion.

# L.T. Woody

Raised in Baltimore, Maryland, L.T. Woody is the author of the memoir, IN BLACK IN WHITE, a coming-of-age story that journeys from the tough streets of West Baltimore, to the ivy-covered Halls of a New England boarding school. Woody worked for the Early Head Start program at The Children's Hospital of Philadelphia (CHOP), and now works for Focus on Fathers; Woody's focus is on families. He graduated from Temple University and enjoys playing guitar and songwriting. He has written more than fifty original songs; writes for Newsworks.org, and has written a theatrical play called Rockaway.

## Mario D. King

Born and raised in Memphis, Tennessee, and now residing in Charlotte, North Carolina Mario is the owner and operator of MDK Entertainment and the author of the hit hip-hop novel The Crisis Before Midlife. An advocate for literacy Mario graduated from the University of Tennessee *at Chattanooga* and received an MBA from Kaplan University. He won the "Poet of the Year" and "Shakespeare Trophy of Excellence" in 2002, and the Black Writers And Book Clubs "Author of the Year" award in 2013.

## RYCJ

A storyteller from birth, born to a family of oral historians, Rhonda Y. C. Johnson determined at an early age she would become a writer. She has written, illustrated and published twenty-two books in a mosaic of genres, from a collection of short stories and poetry to several novels and memoirs. In 2008, she founded OSAAT Entertainment, a fiction and children's book publishing company, and adopted the pen name RYCJ. She's also an avid blogger and reader having reviewed over 300 books.

# Thank You

Odes of praise and thanks are due to the soul of our ancestors who not only handed down their stories based on their experiences, but passed on the spirit of storytelling. We thank those that continue to touch the minds and spirits of readers in a large and genuine way.

# More Books

CHILDREN'S BOOKS

Kiley's Purple Hat

Learn Colors in Spanish with Pumpkin Bear

Pumpkin Bear and his New Friend

Learn Colors in French with Pumpkin Bear


FICTION

The Daughter of God

Double Dare

Puzzles